T 404626

The Boston Tea Party

By Carol M. Elliott

Contents

Setting the Stage

Teacher Read Aloud	2
Vocabulary	3
Fluency Warm-Up	4
Comprehension Warm-Up	5

Act I
Reader's Theater:

A Boston Teapot	6–11

Intermission   12

Act II
Connected Readings:

View of One Who Was There	13
View of King George	14
View of Samuel Adams	15

Curtain Call   16

Rigby • Saxon • Steck-Vaughn

Setting the Stage
Teacher Read Aloud

In the 1700s, it took about two months to sail a ship between England and the American colonies. The colonists started thinking of themselves as separate from England. England did not allow the colonies to elect a representative to Parliament. So when Parliament wanted to tax the colonies, the colonists didn't like it.

In 1767, Parliament passed a set of taxes called the Townshend Acts. The colonists protested. Some of the protests became violent. In Boston, mobs broke windows of stores where English goods were sold. In 1768, England sent soldiers to Boston. The colonists resented the soldiers.

On March 5, 1770, a crowd started shouting at the soldiers. One of the soldiers fired his gun into the crowd. Then eight more soldiers fired. Five colonists died in what came to be known as the Boston Massacre. Two months later the people of Boston learned that on March 5, Parliament had repealed, or gotten rid of, the Townshend Acts.

In Acts I and II of this book, you will learn more about another protest against English taxes, the Boston Tea Party. At the same time, you will practice your reading. Use the vocabulary and warm-ups on the next three pages to get ready.

Vocabulary

Read and review these vocabulary words to prepare you for reading this book. Say these words to yourself. Then say them each aloud two times.

Disguised—wearing a costume to change the way one looks

Loyal—faithful; devoted

Parliament—a representative body having the power to make laws in England

Rebel—one who fights back against a government or ruler

Shipment—delivery of goods

Unite—to bring together for a common purpose

Volunteer—one who freely chooses to do something

Wharf—a pier or dock where ships may tie up and load or unload goods

VOCABULARY THINK TANK

Are you loyal to your friends? How so?

Fluency Warm-Up:
Reading with Word Accuracy

It is hard to read smoothly and fluently if you do not know the words. Fluent readers read all the words in a story. They learn how to pronounce the words with **accuracy**. They look up unfamiliar words in a dictionary or glossary. If a sentence doesn't make sense, they go back and check that they read all the words correctly.

Remember you need to learn how to pronounce all difficult words, names of people, and names of places. And don't ever skip words.

FLUENCY PRACTICE

Practice reading these sentences aloud. Do not skip words.

1. They did not like "taxation without representation."
2. Samuel Adams was a leader in Boston, Massachusetts.
3. Parliament made laws in England.

Comprehension Warm-Up:
Making Connections

When you think about how one story is like another story, you are **making connections**. You can connect ideas from one book with other things you know.

You can connect what you are reading to another book you have read. You can connect what you are reading to something that has happened to you. You also can connect what you are reading to something happening in the world.

COMPREHENSION TIP

Ask yourself questions like these when you read.

1. How does this story remind me of other stories I've read?
2. How do my feelings compare to this character's feelings?
3. How do the events in this story fit with what I know about the world?

ACT 1 READER'S THEATER

A Boston Teapot

Cast of Characters for 5 players

GRANDMA
KIMIKO
PAUL REVERE
DR. THOMAS YOUNG
SAMUEL ADAMS

GRANDMA: Hello, Kimiko. What are you studying?

KIMIKO: Social Studies. We're reading about the Boston Tea Party. But Grandma, I don't understand it. Why did Indians want to throw tea into Boston Harbor?

GRANDMA: I think you misunderstood what you read. The men who took part in the Boston Tea Party were **disguised** as Indians, but they were really colonists.

KIMIKO: Why were they disguised?

GRANDMA: So they wouldn't get into trouble for destroying the tea. It is one of the best kept secrets of all time. No one knows who all was there.

KIMIKO: Now that sounds interesting. It's hard to keep a secret. Tell me more. Why did they destroy the tea? Didn't they like tea?

GRANDMA *(laughs)*: Yes, they liked tea, but they didn't want to have to pay a tea tax.

Kimiko: But everybody has to pay taxes.

Grandma: Yes, but the difference is today we elect the people who make the laws for things like taxes. We have a say in how things are done, but the colonists did not have a say. They did not like "taxation without representation."

Kimiko: So there were no Americans in **Parliament**?

Grandma: Right, the members of Parliament represented the people of England. But the people in the colonies were not allowed to have someone represent them in Parliament.

Kimiko: I bet the colonists didn't like that.

Grandma: They didn't. But when England needed money, Parliament decided the colonists should pay taxes on tea. Everyone drank tea, so everyone would pay the tax. England decided only one company could bring tea to America, and only special merchants could sell the tea.

Paul Revere *(holding up sign that says "Boston, 1773")*: News has come from New York and Philadelphia. A group calling themselves "The Mohawks" sent a letter to each merchant. It said that anyone who helped with the tea would receive an "unwelcome visit" from the Mohawks.

Samuel Adams: Without tea merchants, there will be no one to receive or sell the tea.

Paul Revere: Yes, so the cities are refusing any **shipments** of tea.

Samuel Adams: We must convince our tea merchants in Boston to do the same.

Dr. Young: That won't be easy. Two of our merchants are sons of the governor. Governor Hutchinson is **loyal** to England.

Kimiko: Let me guess. The colonists couldn't convince the Boston tea merchants, right?

Grandma: No, they couldn't. So the colonists decided to resist and return any shipments of tea.

(Paul Revere holds sign saying "November 28, 1773.")

Samuel Adams *(writing a letter)*: We must join forces. We must **unite** to resist England. England has given us only one choice. We can choose to be slaves of England and accept the tea and the unfair tax. Or we can resist like free people.

FLUENCY TIP

Make sure you know how to pronounce the names of the places in this play. Use a dictionary to help you.

PAUL REVERE *(running in)*: The moment of truth has come. A tea ship named the *Dartmouth* has entered the harbor.

SAMUEL ADAMS: We can't let them unload the tea.

PAUL REVERE: We can put off the unloading for 20 days. Then the officers will step in and force the unloading.

Samuel Adams

SAMUEL ADAMS: We'll need guards on the *Dartmouth*. Get 25 **volunteers** to board the ship each evening. They must prevent any attempt to bring the tea on land.

DR. YOUNG: Yes, and send your letter with the fastest riders. Let's have a meeting as soon as possible.

(Paul Revere holds sign saying "Special Town Meeting.")

SAMUEL ADAMS *(speaking to crowd of thousands)*: We must stop the unloading of the ship. We must refuse to pay the tax. We must not give in to England!

CROWD *(cheering)*: Yes! Yes!

Paul Revere: The owner of the ship says he cannot send the ship back without England's okay. If he did, the British would seize his ship. The King would then own his ship.

Dr. Young: There may be only one way to get rid of the tea. We may have to dump it overboard.

Crowd: Yes!

Samuel Adams: We must try to return the tea first.

Grandma: For the next 16 days, the colonists tried everything they could to return the tea to England. During that time, two more tea ships arrived.

Kimiko: They were running out of time.

Grandma: Yes. They must have been planning the "tea party." On the evening of December 16, 1773, there was another town meeting.

(Paul Revere holds sign saying "Special Town Meeting.")

Paul Revere: If nothing is done, tomorrow the officers will seize the tea and bring it on land. The tax then must be paid.

Dr. Young: I wonder how tea mixes with salt water.

Crowd: Yes!

PAUL REVERE: We must not be seen as a mob. We must not hurt anyone or take anything other than the tea.

CROWD: Boston Harbor a teapot tonight! The Mohawks are coming!

GRANDMA: Suddenly the meeting was over, and a crowd was headed to the **wharf**. Some were disguised as Mohawk Indians and were carrying hatchets.

KIMIKO: My book says they chopped open the tea chests. Then they dumped the tea into the sea.

SAMUEL ADAMS: No one must ever know who was at the tea party. They could hang for this.

DR. YOUNG: Let us think of happier thoughts tonight. Look, the job is nearly done. The crowd is breaking up and going home. A little tea was spilled. That is all.

SAMUEL ADAMS: Yes, but who knows what happens next because of this tea party?

FLUENCY TIP

Don't skip any words. If you did, look them up now since you have read the whole play.

INTERMISSION

Self-Check

Did you read all words with accuracy?

Comprehension Prompters

1. Why did the colonists refuse to pay the tax on tea?
2. Whose side are you on? Parliament's or the colonists? Why?
3. What event in the play reminded you of something in your life?

Actor's Corner

What would you have done if you were living in Boston at the time of the Boston Tea Party? With a partner, discuss what each of you would have done and why.

- Would you have gone to the town meetings?
- Would you have taken part in the "tea party"?
- Would you have watched?

ACT II CONNECTED READINGS

VIEW OF ONE WHO WAS THERE

December 17, 1773

Last night I went to a tea party in Boston Harbor. I dressed as an Indian. I painted my face and hands with coal dust. I carried a small hatchet.

I joined others dressed like me. We marched to the three ships. We took out all the chests of tea. We chopped open the chests. Then we threw them overboard!

We didn't try to find out who was working with us. Each person was a **volunteer**. Each person kept his own secret. Each person took the chance of being found out.

It took about three hours. A large crowd watched. Nothing else on the ships was harmed. Then we all went home.

FLUENCY TIP

Practice pronouncing all the words. Then read smoothly as if you were telling about what you did.

VIEW OF KING GEORGE

March 1774

News has come from the colonies. They say **rebels** threw 342 chests of tea into Boston Harbor! We have tried to find out who took part in this. We want names, so that we can punish these rebels. But no one seems to know. The rebels were **disguised** as Indians!

Since we cannot find men to punish, we will punish the whole city of Boston. They will be sorry for what they did. We will close Boston Harbor until the **shipments** of tea are paid for. We will ban special town meetings. We will give more power to the people who are loyal to me. We will make these colonists realize who is king. We will force these people to be loyal to England!

FLUENCY TIP

Do not skip words. Read all the words as if you were an angry king.

View of Samuel Adams

May 1774

News has come from England. King George and **Parliament** are punishing Boston for the "tea party." They insist that Boston must pay for the destroyed tea. They are closing Boston Harbor to all ships until the tea is paid for.

Next Parliament has made it against the law to hold special town meetings. They have increased the powers of the governor, who is loyal to England. They are appointing all leaders. They refuse to let us choose our own leaders.

The people of Boston did nothing wrong. We tried to send the tea back. England wouldn't allow it. We will fight this punishment. We will not pay for the tea!

The colonies must **unite**! If we work together, we can win.

FLUENCY TIP

Read with confidence, like someone who is sure that what he is doing is right.

CURTAIN CALL

Reread

Go back and reread your assigned Act II reading several more times aloud. Remember to read all words with accuracy. Do not skip words. The more you practice, the better reader you will become!

Comprehension Prompters

1. "View of One Who Was There": What would you ask a person who was at the Boston Tea Party?
2. Connect "View of King George" to page 2. Why did it take two months before King George found out about the Boston Tea Party?
3. "View of Samuel Adams": Why did Parliament make it against the law for the colonists to hold meetings?

Taking It Further

With a partner, do some research on what it was like to live in Boston in the 1770s. What kinds of jobs did people have? What did they wear? What did they eat? Present your findings to the class.